Cover illustration: An immaculate Sopwith Camel training machine, its role suggested by the absence of armament. Evident in this photograph are the engine-turned metal cowl and adjacent panels, polished plywood around the cockpit, PC10 Khaki-doped uppersurfaces and clear-doped linen undersides. B6266 was a Sopwith-built machine. (J. M. Bruce/G. S. Leslie Collection)

1. Air-to-air photographs of First World War aircraft are rare, and here is one of the finest of the few left to posterity. This FE2b emphasizes the exposed and quite hazardous position of the observer/gunner in the front cockpit. FE2bs proved more than a match for the Fokker monoplanes in early 1916 on fighter/reconnaissance duties over the Western Front, and eight RFC squadrons operated the type. (RAF Museum)

The Royal Flying Corps
in World War One

RAYMOND LAURENCE RIMELL

ARMS AND ARMOUR PRESS

London – Melbourne – Harrisburg. Pa. – Cape Town

Introduction

Published in 1985 by Arms and Armour Press,
Lionel Leventhal Limited, 2-6 Hampstead High
Street, London NW3 1QQ; 11 Munro Street, Port
Melbourne 3207, Australia; Sanso Centre,
8 Adderley Street, P.O. Box 94, Cape Town 8000,
South Africa; Cameron and Kelker Streets, P.O.
Box 1831, Harrisburg, Pennsylvania 17105, USA

British Library Cataloguing in Publication Data:
Rimell, Raymond Laurence
The RFC in World War One.—(Vintage warbirds; 1)
1. Great Britain. *Royal Flying Corps*—History
2. Fighter planes—History   3. World War, 1914–
1918—Aerial operations, British
I. Title   II. Series
940.4'4941   D620
ISBN 0-85368-693-9

Edited and laid out by Roger Chesneau.
Typeset by Typesetters (Birmingham) Limited.
Printed in Italy
by Tipolitografia G. Canale & C. S.p.A. - Turin
in association with Keats European Ltd.

It is fairly safe to state that the true origins of the modern Royal Air Force can be traced back to the date 28 February 1911, when a British Army order was issued decreeing the creation of the Air Battalion of the Royal Engineers. Later, in November of that year, the British Prime Minister, Rt. Hon. Herbert Asquith, asked the standing sub-committee of the Committee of Imperial Defence, chaired by Lord Haldane, to consider the development of an 'efficient aerial service'. After due consideration, the unanimous decision was taken to form a new arm, the Royal Flying Corps, which was to comprise a Naval Wing, a Military Wing and a Central Flying School. On 13 April 1912 the RFC was constituted by Royal Warrant, and one month later, to the day, the Air Battalion and its reserve were assimilated into the RFC's Military Wing.

The RFC was barely two years old when war came; less than four years later, on 1 April 1918, it was, together with the Royal Naval Air Service (formed 1 July 1914), to disappear with the formation of the Royal Air Force. However, despite the RFC's comparatively brief life, its airmen had evolved techniques of photographic reconnaissance and artillery ranging, had perfected air combat tactics (which were to benefit fighter pilots of later generations), and had demonstrated the true value of the aeroplane in the home defence, strategic and long-range bomber roles. Thus today's RAF can be justifiably proud of its traditions, forged over 70 years ago in the world's first air war.

In presenting this album of photographs my aim has been to provide the reader with a selection of less familiar illustrations at the expense, in some cases, of better quality pictures oft-used elsewhere. The reader should also note that, for convenience, the aircraft types are arranged alphabetically rather than chronologically.

For assistance with photographs, I am indebted to fellow Cross and Cockade members J. M. Bruce, G. S. Leslie and B. Robertson, and to Gp. Capt. W. S. O. Randle CBE AFC DFM FRAeS FBIM, R. Mack, D. Roberts and T. Calloway of the RAF Museum. Thanks are also due to Mrs. A. J. Arkell, I. D. Huntley, P. Kirby, the late Capt. I. V. Pyott's family, Air Marshal Sir Frederick Sowrey KCB CBE AFC, Mrs. J. Stilwell and the late D. Whetton. All uncredited photos are from the author's own collection. Finally, I would like to dedicate this book to the memory of the late Gp. Capt. Frederick Sowrey DSO MC AFC.

Raymond Laurence Rimell

◀2
2. Upward-firing Lewis guns on a BE12b of a Home Defence squadron. Note the proximity of the exhaust pipes to the cockpit, the large fuel tank between the struts and the magneto protruding from the fuselage at lower left. (Sir Frederick Sowrey).

▲3

3. Fitted with the 120hp Beardmore engine, the DH1a was a development of the DH1, the first aircraft built by Airco and designed by Geoffrey de Havilland. The DH1a was superior to the FE2b but only a handful saw RFC service: six examples went to the Middle East and 24 DH1/DH1as were allocated to home defence units. (J. M. Bruce/G. S. Leslie Collection)

4. 'British Airmen in France', a 1916 postcard, depicts a DH2 biplane. The RFC's (indeed the world's) first true fighter aeroplane, the DH2 was a 'pusher' aircraft with the engine and propeller *behind* the pilot. In the days before synchronized weapons, such a configuration afforded a clear field ahead for the pilot to operate his machine gun.

▼4

5. DH2 5925 enjoyed a comparatively long service career: it joined No. 24 Squadron in France in February 1916 and was flown back to the UK on 22 May the following year. The aircraft is seen here at Brooklands, its outer interplane struts still bearing traces of the red and white stripes which characterized No. 24's flight markings. (RAF Museum)

6. Despite some shortcomings, the DH2 gave a good account of itself in its operational heyday during 1916. A Victoria Cross was awarded to a DH2 pilot, Maj. L. W. B. Rees of No. 32 Squadron, for an action on 1 July 1916 when, flying 6015, he routed ten German bombers. The machine shown is 7850, at No. 2 Aircraft Depot, Candas. (J. M. Bruce/G. S. Leslie Collection)

▲7

7. Airco's DH3, although fated never to enter production, eventually provided the basis for the later DH10. Seen here is 7744, with two 160hp Beardmore engines driving four-bladed propellers on standard-length shafts, which necessitated cutting away part of the upperwing trailing edge. (RAF Museum)

8. DH4 A7429, a presentation aircraft, served with No. 55 Squadron and was wrecked on 22 August 1917 following air combat. The crew, Lt. Davyes and Lt. Cooke, made a forced landing at Ramscapelle. Under the starboard wing is a 112lb bomb; note also the cut-away upperwing centre-section to afford the pilot greater upward visibility.

9. The standard Eagle VII installation in the DH4 is superbly illustrated in a photo full of fascinating detail. Exhaust styles varied enormously, but that shown was one of the most common. Note the extensive cooling louvres and the feed from the underwing gravity fuel tank. (RAF Museum)

10. A beautiful example of a 200hp-engine DH4. This particular aircraft, D1773, was built by Westland and features the taller Mk. II undercarriage that was to become standard for the type. Designed by Geoffrey de Havilland, the DH4, although a two-seater, was faster than any contemporary fighter in service. (J. M. Bruce/G. S. Leslie Collection)

▼8

9▲   10▼

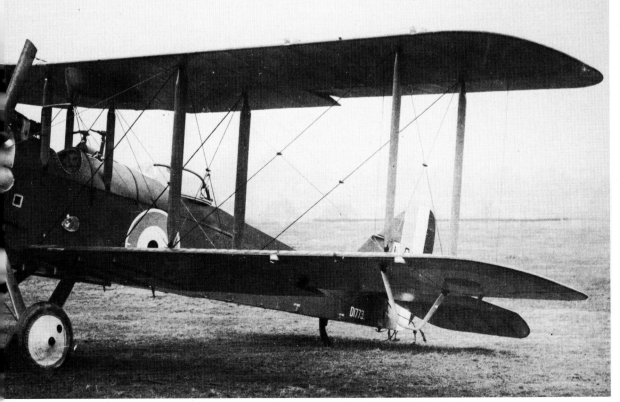

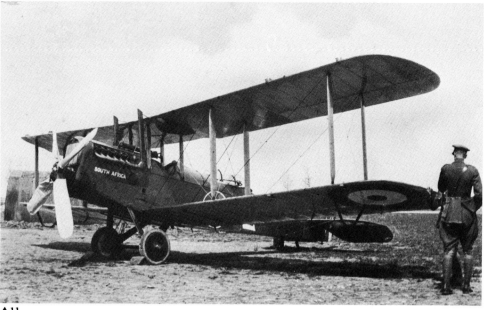

▲11

▲12   ▼13

11. This DH4 was flown by No. 55 Squadron during June 1917 before being transferred to No. 57, in whose service it was destroyed over Ypres on 12 July 1917. The fuselage-mounted Vickers machine gun is clearly seen in this view. Purpose-made canvas covers protect the varnished wood airscrew blades.

12. DH5 A9513 was another presentation machine. The type's distinctive backward stagger was employed so that the pilot's head was directly in line with the upper wing's leading edge and thus afforded a clear view both forward and upward; rearward vision, however, was quite impossible. Unpopular as a 'dogfighter', the DH5 nevertheless gave valuable service in the ground attack role. (J. M. Bruce/G. S. Leslie Collection)

13. The curious DH6 was used in great numbers as a trainer aircraft, and pupils and instructors saddled it with a wide range of service soubriquets such as 'The Clutching Hand', 'The Crab', 'The Skyhook' and 'The Chummy Hearse'. This particular machine is A9580, which served with No. 16 Reserve Squadron at Beaulieu in 1917. (J. M. Bruce/G. S. Leslie Collection)

14. The DH9, powered by the disappointing Puma engine, was intended as a replacement for the DH4 but proved to be inferior. Although over 300 had been built by the end of March 1918, none saw operational service with RFC squadrons, despite units having begun to form with the type around this time. Its powerplant gave poor performance figures and the 'Nine's only real advantage over the DH4 was the close placing of the cockpits, making crew communication much easier.

15. Although not seeing RFC service, the DH9A was a hugely successful type and soldiered on in RAF service until 1931. First produced in 1918 as a DH4 and DH9 replacement, the 'Nine-Ack' was designed around the 400hp Liberty engine, an American powerplant that promised to be a valuable alternative to the Rolls-Royce Eagle. (J. M. Bruce/G. S. Leslie Collection)

16. The Airco DH10 bomber. This is the fourth prototype, C4283, which arrived at Martlesham for testing on 28 July 1918; it had modified engine nacelles and raked wing tips. Known as the 'Amiens', the DH10 saw limited postwar service with No. 97 Squadron in India and No. 216 in Egypt. (J. M. Bruce/G. S. Leslie Collection)

14▲

15▲   16▼

▲17

17. This Armstrong Whitworth FK2 (the initials were those of the designer, Frederick Koolhoven) was the only one of its type to go to France, arriving at St. Omer on 8 September 1915. At that time, the aircraft was powered by a 90hp RAF 1a engine and is seen here at Gosforth with a horn-balanced rudder. Note the fabric-wrapped interplane struts. (J. M. Bruce/G. S. Leslie Collection)

▼18

18. B9572, an Armstrong Whitworth FK3. Records tend to confirm that the only unit to employ the type operationally was No. 47 Squadron in Macedonia, where the FK3 was used for bombing, artillery, observation and contact patrols. The 'Little Ack' saw widespread home use as a trainer, a role which it fulfilled with some success. (J. M. Bruce/G. S. Leslie Collection)

19. 'Big Ack' was the nickname for Armstrong Whitworth's FK8, a rugged, two-seat bomber/reconnaissance machine. The massive exhaust is noteworthy, as are the distinctive side radiators, such features differing from those fitted to standard machines. Two FK8 pilots were awarded the VC – Lt. A. A. McLeod of No. 2 Squadron (27 March 1918) and Capt. F. M. F. West of No. 8 Squadron (10 August 1918).

20. Among the war's more remarkable aircraft were the Armstrong Whitworth FK9 and FK10 (shown) Quadruplanes. Performance figures for the aircraft were poor, and the types featured alarmingly small tailplane units. One of the test pilots reported that the cockpit was so cramped that it was impossible to make full use of the controls. Perhaps mercifully, no quadruplanes entered squadron service. (J. M. Bruce/G. S. Leslie Collection)

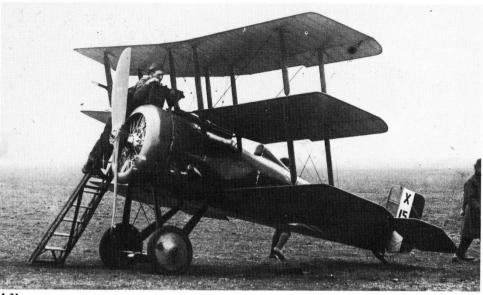

▲21

▲22   ▼23

21. Another experimental type that did not enter production was the Austin AFT3 Osprey, of which three prototypes were planned. While faster than the popular Sopwith Triplane, the Osprey was difficult to land, as one pilot observed: 'When you flattened out the ground was completely obscured, and you had no knowledge to where you were landing at all . . .' The ultimate fate of the prototype X-15 is unrecorded. (J. M. Bruce/G. S. Leslie Collection)

22. Perhaps among the best known aircraft of the period, the Avro 504 and its derivatives had a long and chequered service career. As a fighter, bomber and, universally, a trainer, the 504 was a popular machine with novice and expert alike. E2990 was one of 150 504Ks built by Morgan and Co., whose trademark appears behind the serial on the clear-doped fuselage. (RAF Museum)

23. Avro 504Ks under construction. On the extreme left is an overwing gravity fuel tank, whilst an undercarriage unit lies beyond. Note the glossy sheen of the doped fabric, a finish that soon dulled in service. (RAF Museum).

24. High above a dramatic cloud backdrop, a solitary Avro 504K pursues a leisurely course. The Avro became the RFC's, and later the RAF's, first major training aircraft and continued in service for many years after the Armistice. Several thousands were built.

24▶

▲25

25. An unusual view of an Avro 504K converted for night-fighter use. Note the faired-over forward cockpit, ring-and-bead gun sight and overwing-mounted Lewis machine gun, the muzzle of which can just be seen. Noteworthy, too, are the engine cowling stiffeners and prominent fabric tapes over the wing rib positions. (RAF Museum)

26. The RFC's military two-seat Bleriot XIs were variously powered by 50, 70 and 80hp Gnome rotary engines. The markings of this particular example, 706 (an XI-2), are noteworthy: small Union Flags are doped outboard of the wing cockades, which themselves are of interest since the inner circle is left unpainted. White dope was not always used over clear-doped fabric. (J. M. Bruce/G. S. Leslie Collection)

27. The Bristol biplane of 1910 was a virtual carbon copy of the

Farman, although it did incorporate several structural refinements. The name 'Boxkite' was not its true designation, rather a general nickname applied to a number of similarly-configured machines. Seventy-six Bristol biplanes of this type were built and a handful were still in use as trainers by the RFC when war broke out. (J. M. Bruce/G. S. Leslie Collection)

28. A Bristol Scout D, A1752, in pristine condition and serving with a UK-based training unit. The aircraft is in standard PC10 Khaki camouflage finish, with wing and tail undersurfaces in clear dope (which gave a glossy off-white appearance). Scouts were operated in France, the Aegean and the Middle East, but no British unit was ever exclusively equipped with the type. (J. M. Bruce/G. S. Leslie Collection)

26▲

27▲ 28▼

▲29　▼30

29. Capt. William Leefe Robinson VC stands in front of one of No. 48 Squadron's Bristol F2A Fighters, possibly at Rendcombe in Gloucestershire shortly before the unit left for France. The Bristol's operational debut was hardly an auspicious one: on a patrol over the lines on 5 April 1917, Robinson's flight of six was intercepted by Leutnant Manfred von Richthofen and his pilots of *Jasta 11* and, their new guns jammed, four Bristols were brought down. (Sir Frederick Sowrey)

30. A famous aircraft and an equally famous pilot: a Bristol F2B of No. 48 Squadron and Flt. Cdr. Major Keith Park, later to achieve fame during the Battle of Britain in 1940 when he commanded 11 Group. Points to note on C814 are the non-standard conical spinner (painted white), shortened exhaust stacks and underwing bomb racks. (J. M. Bruce/G. S. Leslie Collection)

31. From a disastrous beginning, the Bristol Fighter, or 'Biff', went on to redeem itself in no small measure, and students of the first air war generally concede that the Bristol was one of the finest all-round aircraft of the conflict. Note on this unarmed example the prominent lacing of the fuselage fabric panels to assist rapid removal for inspection or repair. (J. M. Bruce/G. S. Leslie Collection)

32. During the latter half of the First World War, Bristol Fighters were used for Home Defence by units around London and the outlying environs to counter the threat of the Gotha bomber raids. Here, 'somewhere over Essex', a F2B of No. 39 HDS in full night-fighter camouflage and configuration flies a daylight patrol. (Mrs. A. J. Arkell)

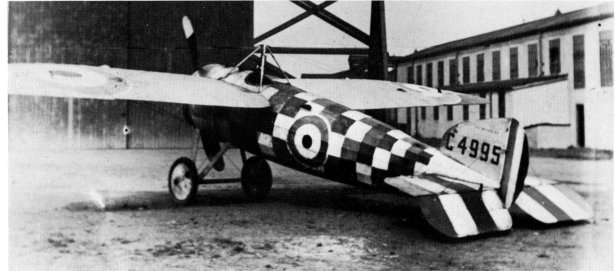

▲33　　　　　▼34

33. Though sorely needed, the Bristol M1C Monoplane did not see Western Front service owing to official disapproval of monoplane designs during early 1917. The type did enjoy limited service in the Middle East, but the majority of those built ended up at training units in the UK. C4995 was one of these and sports a red, white and blue chequerboard scheme; it is thought to have served with No. 2 School of Aerial Fighting. (S. Cotton via D. Roberts)

34. Posing before a Bristol Monoplane is Maj. James Thomas Byford McCudden VC, one of the RFC's most celebrated and respected fighter pilots. The serial of this Bristol is not confirmed but it may be C4965, which is known to have been at Baizieux during No. 56 Squadron's occupation of that aerodrome in early 1918. (RAF Museum)

35. The Caudron G-3, a French design, saw some service with the RFC in the early part of the war. It was employed in the field primarily as a reconnaissance aircraft, and most examples ended their days in British hands as trainers. It should be noted that the lower booms also acted as rudimentary tailskids! (J. M. Bruce/G. S. Leslie Collection)

36. Best known of the French Henry Farman series, the F-20 first appeared in the summer of 1912. For its day the HF F-20 was a successful type, and at the outbreak of war several were on the strength of Nos. 3 and 5 Squadrons, others serving as trainers at the Central Flying School. In the latter role, some examples were known to be in active use as late as October 1917. (J. M. Bruce/G. S. Leslie Collection)

37. Of the many training aircraft used during the war by the RFC, one of the best known was the Maurice Farman Série 7 (Longhorn). It was generally a viceless and forgiving aircraft – ideal for its role – and the deceptively fragile looking structure actually absorbed much of the shock of crash landings which were commonplace in its training capacity. (J. M. Bruce/G. S. Leslie Collection)

35▲

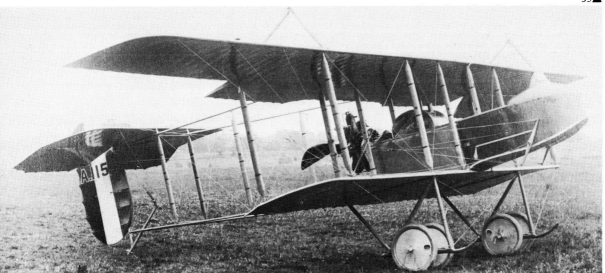

36▲ 37▼

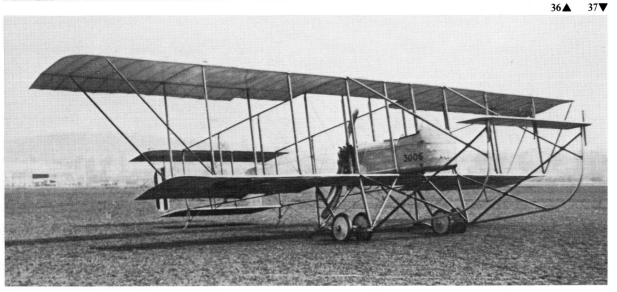

▲38

▲39　▼40

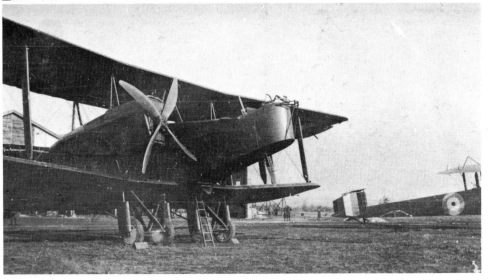

38. No. 498 was a Longhorn of the later, and more numerous, form, with its straight-line lower tail unit and straight tailbooms. This particular machine was still in operation at Netheravon as late as May 1916. (J. M. Bruce/ G. S. Leslie Collection)

39. The Maurice Farman Série 11 was virtually an MF7 without the forward elevator and was, unsurprisingly, known as the 'Shorthorn'. Later examples, such as the aircraft shown here, had kingposts mounted above the upper wings and wire cable bracing to add support to the extensions. (RAF Museum)

40. The No. 1 School of Navigation and Bomb Dropping at Stonehenge in Wiltshire is the background for this pair of Handley Page O/100 bombers. The Royal Flying Corps never used the O/100 or later O/400 operationally, but the type formed the basis for the first heavy bomber squadrons of the newly established Royal Air Force.

41. An HP O/400 under construction. Most obvious in this view is the partially external fuselage fuel tank and the plywood nose panels; also seen here are the Scarff ring for the forward Lewis guns and the tubular mountings for the Rolls-Royce Eagle engines. This photo is dated 12 August 1918. (RAF Museum)

41▶

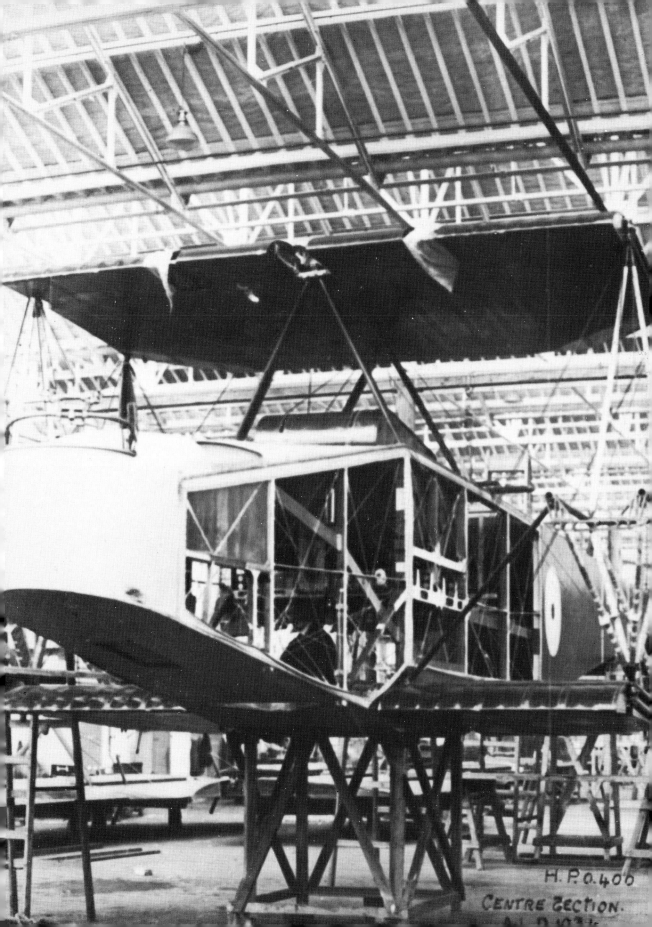

H.P.O.400
CENTRE SECTION

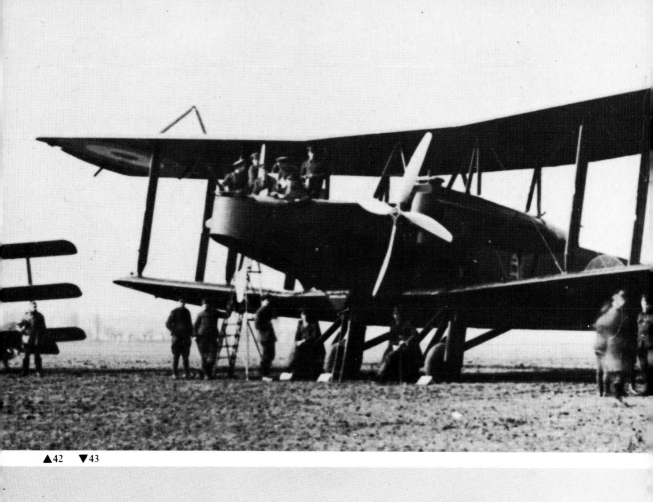

▲42 ▼43

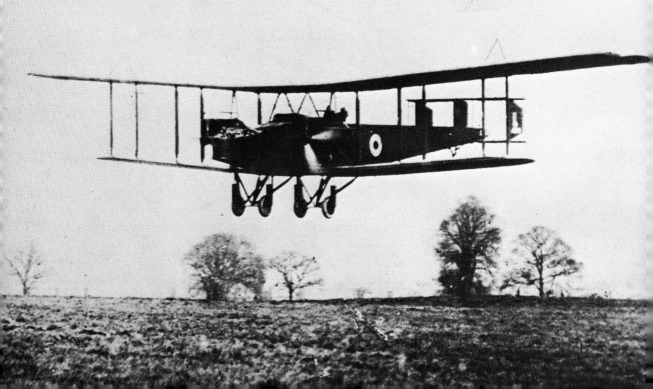

42. A Handley Page O/100 dwarfs the Sopwith Triplane and Nieuport single-seat fighters beside it, the large wing roundels and full rudder stripes marking this aircraft as one of the early examples of 'The Bloody Paralyser'. On later machines, including the O/400, roundels and fin flashes were kept to much smaller proportions for night-bombing operations. (J. M. Bruce/G. S. Leslie Collection)

43. A Handley Page O/400 from an unidentified unit, in night-bomber finish of overall Khaki, comes into land. Note the prominent 'hump' on the upper fuselage between front and rear cockpits (additional fuel tankage) and the red/blue roundel and small-area fin flash. After the Armistice many O/400s were converted to airliners.

44. The Martinsyde S1 was an attractive little biplane, somewhat similar in appearance to the Sopwith Tabloid. This aircraft, 5452, was used at Netheravon as a trainer, possibly with No. 7 Reserve Squadron. In this photograph, the pilot is Lt. C. F. A. Portal, later to become Marshal of the Royal Air Force Lord Portal of Hungerford. (J. M. Bruce/G. S. Leslie Collection)

44 ▼

▲45

45. A Martinsyde S1 is refuelled preparatory to a flight as its heavily garbed pilot looks on. S1s were never numerous in France and pilots complained of the type's poor stability with little aileron control. The aircraft in the background is an Avro 504.

46. Seen here in typical Middle Eastern surroundings is a Martinsyde Elephant. The aircraft was conceived as a long-range escort fighter and reconnaissance platform. On the Western Front, however, only No. 27 Squadron was completely equipped with the type; to this day, the unit crest bears the image of an elephant. (RAF Museum).

47. The Martinsyde F4 Buzzard is considered by most air historians to have been the ultimate First World War fighter aircraft. Had this high-performance machine seen operational service it would have made a great impact on the air war, for it was superior in all respects to every other contemporary British fighter type. (S. Cotton via D. Roberts).

47 ▼

▲48

▲49 ▼50

48. Martinsyde Buzzard B1492, one of four F3s allocated to Home Defence units in 1918. This particular machine was on the strength of No. 141 Squadron for a time and wears typical night-fighting insignia with all-white areas deleted. (Mrs. A. J. Arkell)

49. Another French design which saw RFC service was the Morane Saulnier Type L parasol monoplane. This particular aircraft, 5051, was delivered to the 1st Aircraft Park on 12 August 1915 and went to No. 1 Squadron eight days later. Noteworthy is the non-standard four-blade airscrew. (J. M. Bruce/G. S. Leslie Collection)

50. A Morane Saulnier Type N, popularly known as 'The Bullet', shows to advantage the system of deflector plates fitted to the airscrew. This somewhat crude device was reasonably effective as it prevented the wooden blades from being shattered by rounds fired from the machine gun. (J. M. Bruce/ G. S. Leslie Collection)

51. Whilst the French showed little interest in the Morane Saulnier BB, both the RFC and the RNAS made some use of it. In service, the BB was usually armed with two Lewis guns, and over 80 were eventually delivered to the Corps; its derivation from the Type N is not difficult to appreciate. (J. M. Bruce/G. S. Leslie Collection)

52. A Nieuport 12 two-seater built by Beardmore. Points of interest include the Cellon-covered centre-section to afford the pilot an upward view and the non-standard inboard location for the underwing roundels. RFC Nieuport 12s were mostly transferred from the RNAS. (J. M. Bruce/G. S. Leslie Collection)

53. B1659, a Nieuport 17 or 23 (the types are virtually indistinguishable). The RFC made good use of this little single-seat French fighter, and among its more notable exponents were Ball, Bishop and Mannock. The Nieuports were delivered to the Corps in mid-July 1916 and were still very much in evidence a year later until units began to be equipped with the SE5. (RAF Museum)

51▲

52▲   53▼

▲ 54

54. Another Nieuport type used by the RFC was the 24C.1. This machine, N4662, was photographed shortly after its arrival at No. 2 Aircraft Depot, Candas, where it became B3601 in British service. Issued to No. 40 Squadron on 15 August 1917, it subsequently went to No. 29 in March 1918 and was lost on 7 April whilst being flown by Lt. A. G. Wingate-Grey on a 'special mission'. As with most factory-fresh Nieuports, it sports an overall aluminium doped finish. (J. M. Bruce/G. S. Leslie Collection)

55▲

55. As BE2as came off the production line they were quickly allocated to the Military Wing. In prewar service they saw extensive use in Nos. 2 and 4 Squadrons, with reasonable dependability. In the background of this picture can be seen a Maurice Farman 'Longhorn'. (J. M. Bruce/G. S. Leslie Collection)

56. BE2a 273, seen here at Castle Kennedy, was on the strength of No. 2 Squadron prior to the outbreak of war in August 1914. This particular machine carries no markings of any kind apart from the stark black serial number on its rudder. Note the capacious (and draughty!) cockpit areas. (J. M. Bruce/G. S. Leslie Collection)

56▼

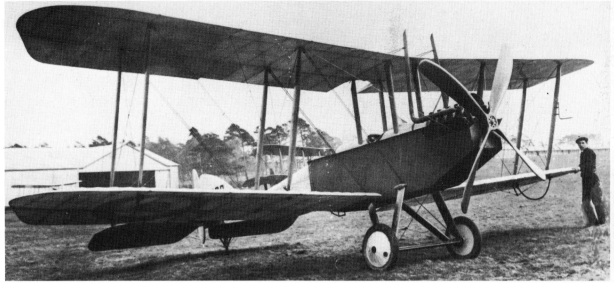

▲57

57. A photograph believed to depict 2028, one of several BE2as that were fitted with heavy armour plating around the nose and forward fuselage. This machine was issued to No. 6 Squadron from No. 2 AD on 9 September 1916 and flew back to England from France on 23 March 1917 and again three months later. Note the absence of white dope on the underwing roundels.

58. The aircraft repair shop at Marske, showing mainplanes being stripped and overhauled; in the foreground a wing panel is being prepared for covering with fabric. Compared with the warplanes of later generations, the machines of the First World War were simple to maintain and repair. (P. Liddle via J. M. Bruce/G. S. Leslie Collection)

59. Lt. Tempest, Capt. Bowers and Lts. Sowrey and Durston stand before BE2c 4112 of B Flight, No. 39 HDS, at Suttons Farm, Hornchurch, in 1916. On 23 September, Lt. Frederick Sowrey was flying 4112 when he destroyed the German Naval Zeppelin *L32* over Billericay, Essex. In the end hangar can be seen a row of Crossley tenders, standard ground equipment for most RFC units. (Sir Frederick Sowrey)

60. The aircraft sheds at Suttons Farm aerodrome at Hornchurch in Essex, home of B Flight, No. 39 HDS, during 1916. The foremost machine hangared (the tail unit is just visible) is Sowrey's famous BE2c 4112, an aircraft which is still in existence in Canada. Note the hangar 'doors' – simple canvas affairs. (Sir Frederick Sowrey)

▼58

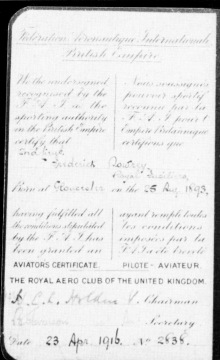

▲61

▲62

61. Frederick Sowrey's Aero Club Certificate 2838, dated 23 April 1916. On the reverse of the right-hand page is printed, in six languages, 'The Civil, Naval and Military authorities, including the Police, are respectfully requested to aid and assist the holder of this certificate'. (Sowrey Family)

62. The Leyland Subsidy A Type Lorry was used in great numbers by the RFC and later by the RAF, so much so in fact that the vehicle generally became known as the Leyland 'RAF Type'. These three-ton trucks were vital equipment in a war theatre where units often had to be rapidly redeployed at a moment's notice. (RAF Museum)

63. This standard Royal Aircraft Factory-engined BE2c, in overall clear-doped finish, sports the increased-area fin style adopted for later-production examples. BE2cs were turned out in massive quantities long after their operational usefulness was over. Only as home-based night-fighters did they achieve any measure of fame.

64. Another fine example of the BE2c, with the uppersurfaces of wings and tailplane in PC10 Khaki dope; the same machine's tail is seen in the previous illustration. The metal engine cowlings are painted in pale grey, and the tips of the lower wings appear to carry Holt night-landing flares.

65. Good close-up cockpit views of 1916 night-fighter aircraft are rare; even rarer is this photo of Lt. William Leefe Robinson's BE2c 2693 in which he destroyed the German airship *SL11* over Cuffley on 3 September 1916. Note the special gun mounting, landing-lamp switches and cartridge flare holder. (J. M. Bruce/G. S. Leslie Collection)

66. A BE2c flies over the trenches in 1915. Practically useless for combat, the BE2c was nevertheless the ideal reconnaissance platform (as was its designer's intention), but as a result of its selection for quantity production it long outlived its useful service life. German pilots took a heavy toll in the skies over the Western Front.

67. A BE2c from an unidentifiable unit flies over a derelict windmill in an unusual and evocative study. About two dozen contractors were responsible for the 1,308 BE2c and BE2d aircraft eventually delivered to the RFC. As a result of various production problems, service entry was delayed until 15 April 1915, when No. 8 Squadron's BE2cs went to war. (RAF Museum)

▲65 ▼66   67▶

▲68

68. An assembly shop, laden with BE tailplanes and wings, probably at the Royal Aircraft Factory at Farnborough. What present-day restorer of vintage aircraft would not give his eye teeth to enter a store like this!

▼69▪

69. RFC carpenters hard at work constructing wing panels; note the stack of interplane struts at the far left. The men in the foreground are working on the wing ribs of a BE-type mainplane whilst in the background other carpenters are planing timber for wing spars.

70. Lt. Frederick Sowrey DSO prepares for a night patrol in BE2e A1855. The aircraft is in full night camouflage: PC10 Khaki, white circles in the roundel positions, and the blue and red areas overpainted. Note the underwing bomb racks (fully laden), wingtip lights and Holt landing flares. (Sir Frederick Sowrey)

71. A Bristol-built BE2e, distinguishable from the 2c by its single-bay wings of unequal span. This splendid photograph reveals useful detail and noteworthy features: fuselage and wing bomb racks; strut transfer logos; stylized fuselage numeral; non-standard spinner; and protective plating around the forward cockpit.

▲72

72. Royal Aircraft Factory BE8 625 was the second of two machines built for India by Vickers and is seen here wearing a somewhat roughly applied non-standard camouflage. It left the Farnborough factory on 11 August 1914 and went to No. 3 Squadron three days later. On 16 August it crashed at Amiens, killing its crew. (RAE via J. M. Bruce/G. S. Leslie)

73. A Home Defence BE12, serial unknown, fitted with five pairs of Le Prieur electrically fired rockets for anti-Zeppelin purposes. As such, the rockets were a dismal failure and pilots, justifiably, put greater reliance on incendiary bullets. Though intended to succeed the BE2c, the BE12 had a performance only marginally superior. (RAF Museum)

▼73

74. An FE2b gunner shows one of the stances he might be required to adopt in a combat situation. The Lewis gun is attached to a No. 4 Mk. III mounting, officially obsolete by mid-1916, and the rear unit is a No. 10 Mk. I Anderson arch mounting with 'swan-neck' sliding telescopic tube. Twin-yoked Lewis guns could be fitted, but these were not common. (RAF Museum)

75. FE2b A5518, showing the simplified undercarriage devised by

Lt. Trafford Jones of No. 20 Squadron. This particular aircraft is a presentation machine, one of hundreds built by subscription from patriotic individuals and overseas countries of the Empire. The nacelle front bears the inscription 'Presented by the Colonies of Mauritius No. 15' painted in white over the standard Khaki finish. (P. Wilson/P. Liddle via J. M. Bruce/G. S. Leslie)

▲76

▲77

▲78

79▶

76. Behind enemy lines: FE2b 7691 of No. 11 Squadron, shot down on 21 March 1917 by *Lt.* Kurt Wolff. The white nose markings are noteworthy, as are the canvas bags on the Lewis gun designed to catch expended cartridges from the circular ammunition drum. The stock for the Lewis was not a common feature. (D. Whetton)

77. Truing up an FE2 airframe. The complex structure and frail appearance of the 'Fee' is somewhat deceptive. This pusher biplane, in all its various derivations, was a workhorse of the RFC, and despite its cumbersome aspect it could, if expertly crewed, prove more than a match for Fokker monoplane fighters.

78. FE8 6456 of No. 40 Squadron was shot down by Kurt Wolff on 9 March 1917. The British pilot was 2nd Lt. T. Shepard, Royal Warwicks, attached RFC. The machine appears not to be camouflaged and the serial number is borne on a white rudder panel. (D. Whetton)

79. In FE8 7616, Lt. Stephen Hay of No. 41 Squadron patrols the air over the Ypres Salient on 2 January 1917. To the type fell the dubious honour of being the last single-seat pusher fighter to see wartime service, although it flew on in the trainer role for some time after its front-line withdrawal. (RAF Museum)

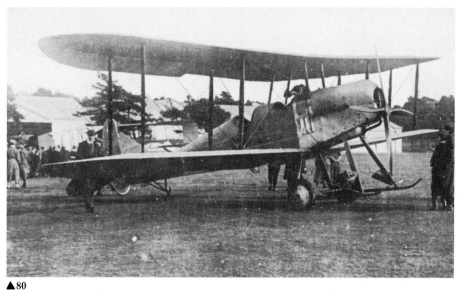

▲80

▲81 ▼82

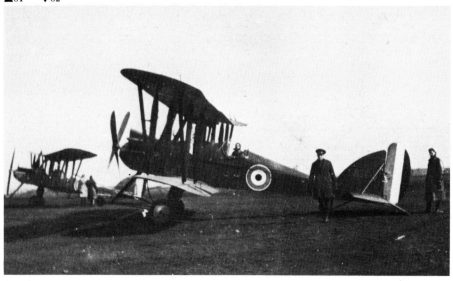

80. The RE5 was described by one pilot as a 'blowzy old woman' that 'floundered about the sky in a safe if unattractive manner'. True, it was not one of the Royal Aircraft Factory's greatest products, but it did contribute significantly to the development of heavy bombing aircraft. Capt. J. A. Liddell of No. 7 Squadron earned the VC flying a RE5. (J. M. Bruce/G. S. Leslie Collection)

81. A standard production RE7, built at the Coventry Ordnance Works (COW), and fitted with a 120hp Beardmore engine. The performance of this ungainly machine was disappointing and the aircraft was condemned by Lt.Col. Hugh Trenchard, GOC of the RFC, as 'useless in the field'. Modern pilots may note that the RE7, with its wing span of 57ft and all-up weight of 3,449lb, had little more power than a Tiger Moth. (J. M. Bruce/G. S. Leslie Collection)

82. RE7 2194, fitted with an RAF 4a engine; the over-generous cockpit may be noted. Various powerplants were fitted to the RE7, and it was only with the installation of a 250hp Rolls-Royce Mk. III in a three-seat version of the aircraft that the latter showed promise; however, the early crash of RE7 2299, and dire need of Rolls-Royce engines elsewhere, spelt the end for the type. (RAF Museum)

83. RE8 A3570, built by Daimler, at Huntingdon in 1917. Known as the 'Harry Tate', after a music hall personality of the time, the RE8 was used widely on the Western Front, in Italy, in Palestine and in Mesopotamia as a reconnaissance, artillery-spotting and bombing aircraft. Over 2,260 had been delivered to the RFC by March 1918.

84. RE8s undergoing overhaul in Huntingdon's hangars. Note that the machine in the background has the greatly enlarged tailfin which was fitted to the many training RE8s. Also of interest, on the middle aircraft, is the non-standard small centre spot of the lower wing roundel.

83▲   84▼

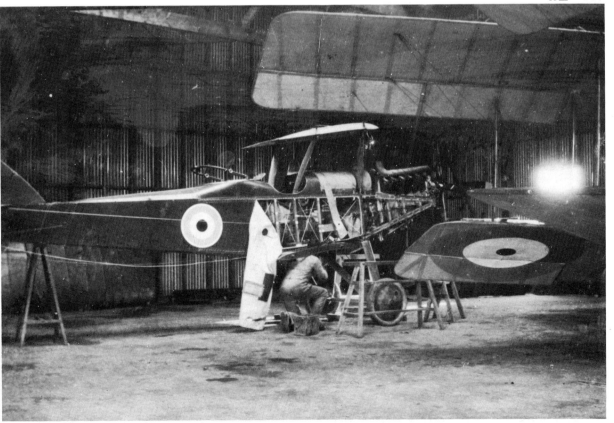

▲85

86▲

85. A SE5 of No. 56 Squadron at London Colney, April 1917, showing the semi-enclosed cockpit canopy which was discarded by pilots because of its constrictive nature – an amusing paradox to modern eyes. Note that this aircraft is not fitted with a headrest and carries an overwing gravity tank. The item hanging from the cockpit is a waist safety harness. (J. M. Bruce/G. S. Leslie Collection)

86. A famous air VC: Capt. Albert Ball, typically *sans* helmet and goggles, seated in SE5 A4850 at London Colney, Hertfordshire, on 7 April 1917, prior to No. 56 flying out to France. Note the standard windscreen which replaced the bulky 'glasshouse' of the type as delivered, and the creased appearance of the removable fuselage side panel. (J. M. Bruce/G. S. Leslie Collection)

87. No. 56 Squadron's SE5 aircraft at London Colney aerodrome in April 1917. The machines all feature the semi-enclosed cabins that pilots disliked so much. Note that headrests are not universally fitted and that the upperwing roundels lack the usual thin white surround. (J. M. Bruce/G. S. Leslie Collection)

87▼

88. The experimental camouflage applied to this SE5a night-fighter of a Home Defence unit provides a surreal appearance. Note that the roundels and rudder stripes have had their white areas painted out. The colours are not known, but the diamonds may be of a light grey dope over the basic PC10 Khaki finish. (J. M. Bruce/G. S. Leslie Collection)

89. Another famous RFC airman. Capt. William Avery Bishop VC, a Canadian, was one of the most successful fighter pilots of the war. Unlike many of the top airmen, he survived the conflict, and he enjoyed a long career in the RCAF, in which he served as an air marshal during the Second World War. (J. M. Bruce/G. S. Leslie Collection)

90. The standard armament of SE5a B4899, with ring-and-bead sights on the Vickers gun; the Aldis optical sight is not fitted, but the circular mounting brackets can be seen on the right. Prominent on the dashboard is the wooden container for a spare 97-round ammunition drum for the overwing Lewis gun. (T. Hefferman via J. M. Bruce/G. S. Leslie).

91. (Next spread) SE5a C6414 nears completion at the Wolseley plant. This view affords a rare glimpse of the Wolseley Viper engine installation and of the rear fuselage structure before the fabric panel is laced. The SE5a succeeded the SE5 into RFC service and was flown by most of Britain's leading airmen. (J. M. Bruce/G. S. Leslie Collection)

▲92   ▼93

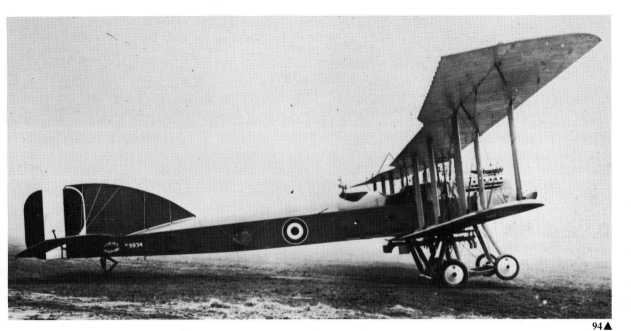

94▲

92. Mass production: SE5as being built at the Wolseley works in Birmingham. Seen here in various stages of construction, the airframes may appear fragile to modern eyes, but they were in fact surprisingly sturdy. Large cut-outs in front of the cockpits provided access to the offset Vickers machine gun. (J. M. Bruce/G. S. Leslie Collection)

93. Another home defence SE5a, with grey diamonds over the Khaki finish. Whilst very successful in France, the SE5a was not well suited to night flying, its landing speed being considered rather too high. Noteworthy in this photograph are the absence of fuselage roundels, the flame-damped exhaust and the commander's strut pennants. (J. M. Bruce/G. S. Leslie Collection)

94. The Short Bomber was conceived as a 'stop-gap', pending production of the Handley Page O/100, for the RNAS, which wanted to press home attacks on German naval installations. Twenty Shorts were transferred to the RFC, but they were not used operationally in France. (J. M. Bruce/G. S. Leslie Collection)

95. A standard Sopwith LCT (Land Clerget Tractor) 1½ Strutter with Scarff ring mounting on the rear cockpit. The type was built in both single- and twin-seat configuration and enjoyed lengthy service in both the RFC and the RNAS. It was the first two-seat fighter to carry a synchronized forward-firing machine gun. (J. M. Bruce/G. S. Leslie Collection)

95▼

▲96   ▼97

▼98

96. A superb study of A977, a Westland-built Sopwith 1½ Strutter. Close scrutiny reveals plenty of interesting details: the padded windscreen behind the Vickers gun; the Scarff ring; the external control cables; and the Cellon-covered centre-section. (I. D. Huntley)

97. Generally regarded by most contemporary pilots as the ultimate flying machine, the Sopwith Pup was one of the RFC's most successful early war fighters, despite its single-gun armament. This unarmed machine is probably a trainer; students of markings may note that the wheel covers are painted over in red, white and blue as a cockade. (RAF Museum)

98. Sopwith Pup B5343 comes to grief on a snow-covered airfield following a landing mishap. This particular Pup was built by Whitehead Aircraft in their B5251–B5400 batch; it is finished in the standard colour scheme for the period, with a fuselage band in blue and white. (RAF Museum)

99. A factory-fresh Pup with extensive use of Cellon covering across the centre-section. Points to note are the picket rings under the lower wing (just beneath the forward interplane struts), 'engine-turned' riffling on the metal nose panels and cowling, and the glossy appearance of a new aircraft. (J. M. Bruce/G. S. Leslie Collection)

99 ▼

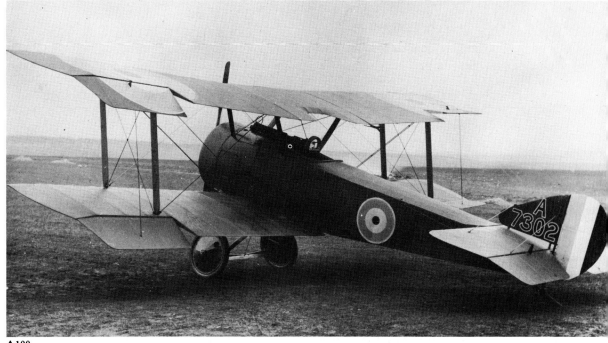

▲100

100. Sopwith Pup A7302 was built by Standard Motors of Coventry. There is no upper wing cut-out, and the engine cowling and metal panels are overpainted. The splayed-out wheels are characteristic of machines featuring the bungee-sprung split axle undercarriage. (J. M. Bruce/G. S. Leslie Collection).

101. The Sopwith Triplane appeared soon after the Pup. With a more powerful engine, the triplane's handling qualities were extremely good and for the time its climb rate was nothing short of phenomenal. Both RFC and RNAS orders were forthcoming, but inter-service policy changes led to these being reduced and the type served operationally only with the RNAS. One machine, N5430, was evaluated by the RFC at Martlesham Heath. (RAF Museum).

102. One of the most prized exhibits at the RAF Museum is the superbly restored twin-gun Shuttleworth and Clayton-built Sopwith Triplane N5912. This photograph shows what the aircraft looked like as an unarmed trainer, complete with large numerals on fuselage and wings. (S. Cotton via D. Roberts).

103. Together with the German Fokker Triplane, the Sopwith Camel shares the distinction of being the best-known fighter of the First World War. This presentation machine, E1548, was built by Ruston Proctor and Co. Ltd. of Lincoln and served with No. 65 Squadron. It was shot down on 9 August 1918, the pilot, Lt. C. W. Illingworth, being made a prisoner-of-war. (J. M. Bruce/G. S. Leslie Collection).

▼101

102▲ 103▼

104. A Sopwith Camel of No.
46 Squadron, carrying four
Cooper bombs under the fuselage. Camels served in most war
theatres and were used in Bel-
gian, Greek and American
squadrons as well as in the
RFC, the RNAS and, later, the
RAF. Not an easy aeroplane to
fly, the Camel was nevertheless
one of the finest combat aircraft
of its day. (J. M. Bruce/G. S.
Leslie Collection)

105. An unusual view of the
Sopwith F1 Camel's standard
armament, a pair of synchronized Vickers .303 machine
guns. Note the style of windscreen (there were wide varia-
tions of pattern) and the closely
grouped cockpit instruments.
(J. M. Bruce/G. S. Leslie
Collection)

106. Another famous pilot –
another famous aircraft. Maj.
William George Barker DSO MC,
commanding officer of No. 139
Squadron RAF, and his 'spe-
cial' Sopwith Camel B6313.
Barker joined the RFC in De-
cember 1915 and later won the
VC for a single-handed action
involving a large number of
German fighters. (J. M. Bruce/
G. S. Leslie Collection)

107. Another unusual view of
the peppery little Camel, showing one of its more distinctive
recognition features – the upper
mainplane's zero-dihedral. Just
as interesting is the background
of this picture, which shows
Camels in various stages of construction. Note the rolls of linen
covering material at the extreme
top left. (J. M. Bruce/G. S.
Leslie Collection)

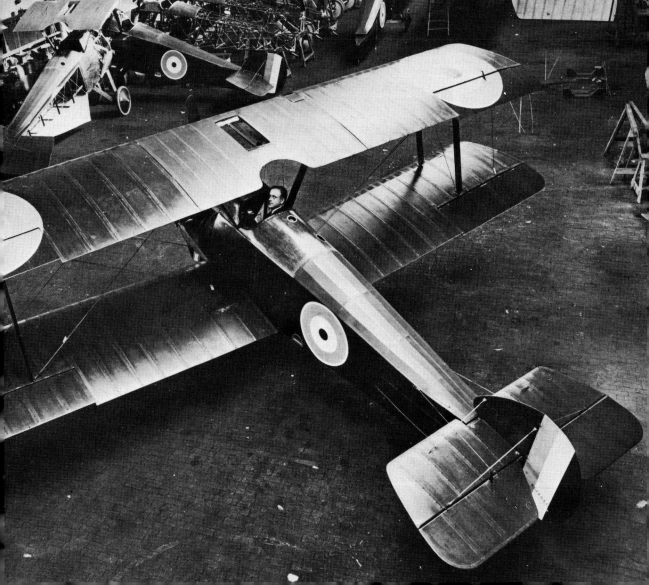

▲108 ▼109

108. A Sopwith Camel undergoing maintenance; the engine is a Clerget. Note the channel in the firewall to exhaust gases out and downwards away from the fuselage. At the extreme right can be seen two simple toolboxes, a far cry from the sophisticated back-up required for today's warplanes. (J. M. Bruce/G. S. Leslie Collection)

109. A Sopwith 7F1 Dolphin of No. 79 Squadron in RAF service. Introduced in 1917, this single-seater was the world's first four-gun fighter, although the full complement was rarely carried in operational service. Contemporary reports of the Dolphin speak highly of its qualities but its somewhat unorthodox appearance and exposed pilot's position made it unpopular. (J. M. Bruce/G. S. Leslie Collection)

110. The first SPAD 7 to be delivered to the RFC was allocated the serial number A253 and is seen here at No. 2 AD, Candas, shortly after its arrival. Issued to No. 60 Squadron on 20 September 1916, it returned to Candas the following month and was later sent back to the UK. It was still flying in July 1918, with No. 56 Training Squadron. The word 'SPAD' was a contraction of 'Société Anonyme pour l'Aviation et ses Dérivés. (J. M. Bruce/G. S. Leslie Collection)

111. The SPAD 13 formed the full complement of only one RFC unit, No. 23 Squadron, replacing the latter's SPAD 7s during December 1917. The Corps claimed no spectacular successes with the type during its four months of squadron service, and the SPADs were subsequently returned to Candas. (J. M. Bruce/G. S. Leslie Collection)

112. The Vickers FB5. This particular machine, 1616, was the first production FB5 for the RFC and is seen here at Farnborough in December 1914 with Frank Goodden at the controls. It served with No. 5 Squadron for a while before finally being struck off charge on 20 September 1915. (B. Robertson)

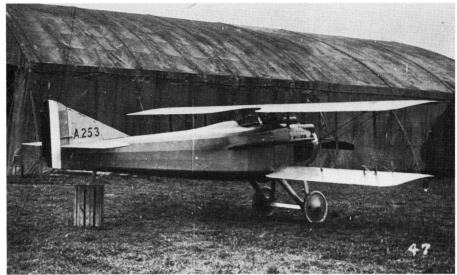

110▲

111▲ 112▼

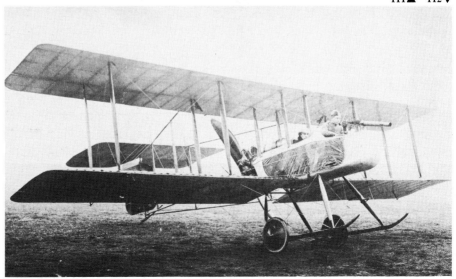

▲113

113. The Vickers ES1 'Scout' saw some operational use with three Western Front squadrons even though only a handful of aircraft were actually built. Two examples, 7754 and 5127, were used by No. 50 HDS at Dover for a time, but there is no record of them ever having been flown in action. (RAF Museum)

114. Towards the end of 1915 Vickers designed and built a somewhat refined version of the FB5. The new aircraft, designated FB9, was ordered in considerable numbers but only a few saw limited service, with No. 11 Squadron during the early phases of the Battle of the Somme. The majority of FB9s ended their days in the trainer role. (J. M. Bruce/G. S. Leslie Collection)

115. The Vickers FB12 was a single-seat pusher in the DH2/FE8

▼114

mould. Various engines were installed in the type, some of which gave the machine a particularly inspiring performance. Shown here is FB12C A7552 (one of the production batch), fitted with a 100hp Anzani. (J. M. Bruce/G. S. Leslie Collection)

116. A8963, the sole example of the Vickers FB16A, was later designated FB16D when fitted with a 20hp Hispano Suiza engine. Capt. J. T. B. McCudden vc flew the type at Joyce Green on 22 June 1917 and was greatly impressed, so much so that he wanted to take the aircraft back to France with him. However, the FB16D never did go to France – nor did it see production. (S. Cotton via D. Roberts)

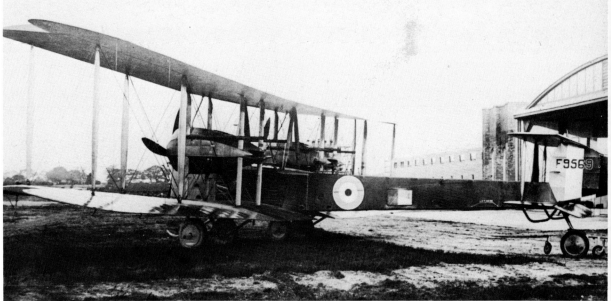

▲117

117. The Vickers FB27 Vimy made its first flight in prototype form at Joyce Green on 30 November 1917 and the RFC ordered 150 on 26 March the following year, but the aircraft arrived too late for RFC use and the first production machine only reached Martlesham Heath for testing some three months after the Armistice. F9569 was one of the 50 or so examples actually delivered. (J. M. Bruce/G. S. Leslie Collection)

118. Tailpiece. Accidents were fairly frequent at training schools and operational units: here, a Sopwith Dolphin and an Avro 504K have come to grief. Note the painted fuselage undersides, the prominent wing rib tapes and the fuel-soaked fabric on the Dolphin's lower wings. (S. Cotton via D. Roberts)

▼118